THE HATRED OF POETRY

Ben Lerner was born in Topeka, Kansas, in 1979. He has received fellowships from the Fulbright, Guggenheim, and MacArthur Foundations, and is the author of two internationally acclaimed novels, *Leaving the Atocha Station* and *10:04*. He has published three poetry collections: *The Lichtenberg Figures, Angle of Yaw*, and *Mean Free Path*. Lerner is a professor of English at Brooklyn College.

Fitzcarraldo Editions

THE HATRED OF POETRY

BEN LERNER

In ninth grade English, Mrs. X required us to memorize and recite a poem, so I went and asked the Topeka High librarian to direct me to the shortest poem she knew, and she suggested Marianne Moore's "Poetry," which, in the 1967 version, reads in its entirety:

I, too, dislike it.
  Reading it, however, with a perfect
    contempt for it, one discovers in
  it, after all, a place for the genuine.

I remember thinking my classmates were suckers for having mainly memorized Shakespeare's eighteenth sonnet, whereas I had only to recite twenty-four words. Never mind the fact that a set rhyme scheme and iambic pentameter make fourteen of Shakespeare's lines easier to memorize than Moore's three, each one of which is interrupted by a conjunctive adverb—a parallelism of awkwardness that basically serves as its form. That, plus the four instances of "it," makes Moore sound like a priest begrudgingly admitting that sex has its function while trying to avoid using the word, an effect amplified by the deliberately clumsy enjambment of the second line and the third ("in / it"). In fact, "Poetry" is a very difficult poem to commit to memory, as I demonstrated by failing to get it right each of the three chances I was given by Mrs. X, who was looking down at the text, my classmates cracking up.

I, too My contempt for the assignment was, after all, imperfect. Even now I routinely misquote the second sentence; I just Googled the poem and had to correct what I typed out above, but who could forget the first? *I, too, dislike it* has been on repeat in my head since 1993; when I open a laptop to write or a book to read: *I, too, dislike it*

8

echoes in my inner ear. When a poet is being introduced (including myself) at a reading, whatever else I hear, I hear: *I, too, dislike it*. When I teach, I basically hum it. When somebody tells me, as so many people have told me, that they don't get poetry in general or my poetry in particular and/or believe that poetry is dead: *I, too, dislike it*. Sometimes this refrain has the feel of negative rumination and sometimes a kind of manic, mantric affirmation, as close as I get to unceasing prayer.

"Poetry": What kind of art assumes the dislike of its audience and what kind of artist aligns herself with that dislike, even encourages it? An art hated from without and within. What kind of art has as a condition of its possibility a perfect contempt? And then, even reading contemptuously, you don't achieve the genuine. You can only clear a *place* for it—you still don't encounter the actual poem, the genuine article. Every few years an essay appears in a mainstream periodical denouncing poetry or proclaiming its death, usually blaming existing poets for the relative marginalization of the art, and then the defenses light up the blogosphere before the culture, if we can call it a culture, turns its attention, if we can call it attention, back to the future. But why don't we ask: What kind of art is defined—has been defined for millennia—by such a rhythm of denunciation and defense? Many more people agree they hate poetry than can agree what poetry is. I, too, dislike it, and have largely organized my life around it (albeit with far less discipline and skill than Marianne Moore) and do not experience that as a contradiction because poetry and the hatred of poetry are for me—and maybe for you—inextricable.

Caedmon, the first poet in English whose name we know, learned the

10

art of song in a dream. According to Bede's *Historia*, Caedmon was an illiterate cowherd who couldn't sing. When, during this or that merry feast, it was decided that everyone in turn would contribute a song, Caedmon would withdraw in embarrassment, maybe claiming he had to go look after the animals. One night, somebody tries to pass Caedmon the harp after dinner, and he flees to the stable. There among the ungulates he drifts off and is visited by a mysterious figure, probably God. "You must sing to me," says God. "I can't," Caedmon says, if not in these words. "That's why I'm sleeping in the stable instead of drinking mead with my friends around the fire." But God (or an angel or demon—the text is vague) keeps demanding a song. "But what should I sing?" asks Caedmon, who I imagine is desperate, cold-sweating through a nightmare. "Sing the beginning of

What should I sing?

11

created things," instructs the visitor. Caedmon opens his mouth and, to his amazement, gorgeous verses praising God pour forth.

The loss of grace

Caedmon awakes as a poet, and eventually becomes a monk. But the poem he sings upon waking is not, according to Bede, as good as the poem he sang in his dream, "for songs, be they never so well made, cannot be turned of one tongue into another, word for word, without loss to their grace and worthiness." If that's true of translation in the waking world, it's doubly true of translation from a dream. The actual poem Caedmon brings back to the human community is necessarily a mere echo of the first.

Allen Grossman, whose reading of Caedmon I'm pirating here, abstracts from this story (and there are many versions of this story) a harsh lesson: Poetry arises from the desire to get beyond the finite and the historical—the

12

human world of violence and difference—and to reach the transcendent or
divine. You're moved to write a poem,
you feel called upon to sing, because of
that transcendent impulse. But as soon
as you move from that impulse to the
actual poem, the song of the infinite
is compromised by the finitude of its
terms. In a dream your verses can defeat time, your words can shake off the
history of their usage, you can repre-
sent what can't be represented (e.g., the
creation of representation itself), but
when you wake, when you rejoin your
friends around the fire, you're back
in the human world with its inflexible
laws and logic.

Thus the poet is a tragic figure. *The virtual*
The poem is always a record of fail- *and the actual*
ure. There is an "undecidable conflict"
between the poet's desire to sing an
alternative world and, as Grossman
puts it, the "resistance to alternative
making inherent in the materials of

which any world must be composed." In an essay on Hart Crane, Grossman develops his notion of a "virtual poem"—what we might call poetry with a capital "P," the abstract potential of the medium as felt by the poet when called upon to sing—and opposes it to the "actual poem," which necessarily betrays that impulse when it joins the world of representation.

Here I am bypassing the beautiful intricacies of Grossman's account to extract from his under-read and almost freakishly brilliant essays the idea that actual poems are structurally foredoomed by a "bitter logic" that cannot be overcome by any level of virtuosity: Poetry isn't hard, it's impossible. (Maybe this helps us understand Moore: Our contempt for any particular poem must be perfect, be total, because only a ruthless reading that allows us to measure the gap between the actual and the virtual will

A bitter logic

enable us to experience, if not a genuine poem—no such thing—a place for the genuine, whatever that might mean.) Grossman speaks to me because, like so many poets, I live in the space between what I am moved to do and what I can do, and confront in that disconnect not only my individual limitations (although I feel those, too) but also the structure of the art as I conceive it. And I reencounter that implicit structure, again and again, in the claims of both those who purport to denounce poetry and those who would rush to its defense.

The bitterness of poetic logic is particularly astringent because we were taught at an early age that we are all poets simply by virtue of being human. Our ability to write poems is therefore in some sense the measure of our humanity. At least that's what we were taught in Topeka: We all have feelings inside us (where are

You're a poet

15

they located, exactly?); poetry is the purest expression (the way an orange expresses juice?) of this inner domain. Since language is the stuff of the social and poetry the expression in language of our irreducible individuality, our personhood is tied up with our poethood. "You're a poet and you don't even know it," Mr. X used to tell us in second grade; he would utter this irritating little refrain whenever we said something that happened to rhyme. I think the jokey cliché betrays a real belief about the universality of poetry: Some kids take piano lessons, some kids study tap dance, but we don't say every kid is a pianist or dancer. You're a poet, however, whether or not you know it, because to be part of a linguistic community—to be hailed as a "you" at all—is to be endowed with poetic capacity.

If you are an adult foolish enough to tell another adult that you are (still!) a poet, they will often describe for you their falling away from poetry: I wrote it in high school; I dabbled in college. Almost never do they write it now. They will tell you they have a niece or nephew who writes poetry. These familiar encounters—my most recent was at the dentist, my mouth propped open while Dr. X almost gagged me with a mirror, as if searching for my innermost feelings—have a tone that's difficult to describe. There is embarrassment for the poet—couldn't you get a real job and put your childish ways behind you?—but there is also embarrassment on the part of the nonpoet, because having to acknowledge one's total alienation from poetry chafes against the early association of poem and self. The ghost of that romantic conjunction makes the falling away from poetry a falling away from the pure potentiality of being human into the vicissitudes of being an actual

A mirror in the mouth

17

person in a concrete historical situation, your hands in my mouth. I had the sensation that Dr. X, as he knocked the little mirror against my molars, was contemptuous of the idea that genuine poetry could issue from such an opening. And Dr. X was right: There is no genuine poetry; there is only, after all, and at best, a place for it.

The awkward and even tense exchange between a poet and non-poet —they often happen on an airplane or in a doctor's office or some other contemporary no-place—is a little interpersonal breach that reveals how inextricable "poetry" is from our imagination of social life. Whatever we think of particular poems, "poetry" is a word for the meeting place of the private and the public, the internal and the external: My capacity to express myself poetically and to comprehend such expressions is a fundamental qualification for social recognition. If

I have no interest in poetry or if I feel repelled by actual poems, either I am failing the social or the social is failing me. I don't mean that Dr. X or anyone else thinks in these terms, or that these assumptions about poetry are present for everyone, let alone in the same degree, or that this is the only or best way of thinking about poetry, but I am convinced that the embarrassment, or suspicion, or anger that is often palpable in such meetings derives from this sense of poetry's tremendous social stakes (combined with a sense of its tremendous social marginalization). And it's these stakes which make actual poems an offense: If my seatmate in a holding pattern over Denver calls *A holding* on me to sing, demands a poem from *pattern* me that will unite coach and first class in one community, I can't do it. Maybe this is because I don't know how to sing or because the passengers don't know how to listen, but it might also

19

be because "poetry" denotes an impossible demand. This is one underlying reason why poetry is so often met with contempt rather than mere indifference and why it is periodically denounced as opposed to simply dismissed: Most of us carry at least a weak sense of a correlation between poetry and human possibility that cannot be realized by poems. The poet, by his very claim to be a maker of poems, is therefore both an embarrassment and accusation.

And when you are foolish enough to identify yourself as a poet, your interlocutors will often ask: A *published* poet? And when you tell them that you are, indeed, a published poet, they seem at least vaguely impressed. Why is that? It's not like they or anybody they know reads poetry journals. And yet there is something deeply right, I think, about this knee-jerk appeal to publicity. It's as if to say: Everybody can write a poem, but has your poetry, the distillation of your innermost being, been found authentic and intelligible by others? Can it circulate among persons, make of its readership, however small, a People in that sense? This accounts for the otherwise bafflingly persistent association of poetry and fame—baffling since no poets are famous among the general population. To demand proof of fame is to demand proof that your songs made it back intact from the dream in the stable to the social world of the fire, that your song is at once utterly specific to you and exemplary for others.

Stable to fire

(At the turn of the millennium, when I was the editor of a tiny poetry and art magazine, I would receive a steady stream of submissions—our address was online—from people who had clearly never read our publication but whose cover letters expressed a remarkable desperation to have their poems printed *anywhere*. Some of these letters—tens of them—explained that the poet in question was suffering from a terminal condition and wanted, needed, to see his or her poems published before he or she died. I have three letters here that contain the sentence, "I don't know how long I have." I also received multiple letters from prisoners who felt poetry publication was their best available method for asserting they were human beings, not merely criminals. I'm not mocking these poets; I'm offering them as examples of the strength of the implicit connection between poetry and the social recognition of the poet's humanity. It's an association so strong that the writers in question observe no contradiction in the fact that they are attempting to secure and preserve their personhood in a magazine that no one they know will see. It is as though the actual poem and publication do not matter;

I don't know how long I have

22

what matters is that the poet will know and can report to others that she is a published poet, a distinction that no-body—not Death, not the social death of exclusion from the Law—can take from her. Poetry makes you famous without an audience, an abstract or kind of proto-fame: It is less that I am known in the broader community than that I know I could be known, less that you know my name than that I know I am named: *I am a poet / and you know it.*)

And when you are foolish enough to identify yourself as a poet, your interlocutor will often ask you to name your favorite poets. When you say, "Cyrus Console," he squints as if searching his memory and nods as if he can almost recall the work and the name, even though of course he can't (none of the hundreds of non-poet acquaintances who have asked you this sort of question ever can). But I have decided—am deciding as I write—that

Who are your favorite poets?

23

I accept that look, that I value it. I love that the non-poet is conditioned to believe that the name and work are almost within reach even though the only poems he's encountered in the last few decades have been at weddings and funerals. I love how it seems like he's on the verge of recalling a specific line before he slowly shakes his head and concedes: I've never heard of him or her; it doesn't ring a bell. Among other things this is a (no more than semiconscious) performance of the demands of poetry, at this point almost a muscle memory: The poem is a technology for mediating between me and my people; the poem must include me, must recognize me and be recognizable—so recognizable I should be able to recall it without ever having seen it, like the face of God.

Exchanges of this sort strike me as significant because I feel they are contemporary descendants, however diminished, of those founding dialogues about poetry that have set, however shakily, the terms for most denunciations and defenses in the West. Plato, in the most influential attack on poetry in recorded history, concluded that there was no place for poetry in the Republic because poets are rhetoricians who pass off imaginative projections as the truth and risk corrupting the citizens of the just city, especially the impressionable youth. (Socrates' questions in *The Republic* are so leading and full of traps that he might as well have his hands in his interlocutors' mouths.) One difference between Plato's Socrates and Dr. X is that Socrates fears and resents the corrupting power of actual poetic performance—he thinks poets are going to excite excessive emotions, for instance—whereas Dr. X presumably fears and resents his inability to be moved by or comprehend what

None shall sing worthily

passes for a poem. Still, Socrates' in-
terrogations of poets—what do they
really know, what do they really contribute—will feel familiar to many of
my contemporaries. Plato/Socrates
is trying to defend language as the
medium of philosophy from the un-
reason of poets who just make stuff
up as opposed to discovering genuine truths. The oft-remarked irony
of Plato's dialogues, however, is that
they are themselves poetic: formally
experimental imaginative dramatiza-
tions. We might say that Socrates ("He
who does not write," as Nietzsche
put it) is a new breed of poet who has
found out how to get rid of poems. He
argues that no existing poetry can express the truth about the world, and his
dialogues at least approach the truth
by destroying others' claims to possess
it. Socrates is the wisest of all people
because he knows he knows nothing; Plato is a poet who stays closest

to Poetry because he refuses all actual poems. Every existing poem is a
lie, and Plato "reads" the claims made
on behalf of those poems and refutes
them in order to promote the endless
dialectical conversation that is reason
over the false representation that is
an actual poem. Socratic irony: perfect contempt. Plato's famous attack on
poets can be read, therefore, as a defense of Poetry from poems. Socrates:
"Of that place beyond the heavens
none of our earthly poets has yet sung,
and none shall sing worthily..."

I remember first reading Plato at the
Topeka and Shawnee County Public
Library and feeling poetry must be a
powerful art if the just city depended
on its suppression. How many poets'
outsized expectations about the political effects of their work, or critics'
disappointment in what actual poems
contribute to society, derive from
Plato's bestowing us with the honor

of exile? Of course, many poets under totalitarian regimes have been banished, or worse, because of their writing; we must honor those—like Socrates himself—who died for their language. But *The Republic*'s attack on poets has helped sponsor for thousands of years the vague notion that poetry has profound political stakes even in contexts where nobody can name a poet or quote a poem. Anybody who reads (or reads the *SparkNotes* for) *The Republic* is imbued with the sense that poetry is a burning social question. When I declared myself a poet, I knew it was an important calling not because I had seen the impact of actual poems, but because the founding figure of the Western tradition was convinced that poets had to go. (The difference between what Socrates and I meant by "poet" or "poem" never occurred to me; the point was my work would be revolutionary; I, like many

28

poets and critics, acquired my idealism via Platonic contempt.)

It didn't stop, of course, with the Greeks. When I read around in the Renaissance, there were more assaults on poetry, the assailants often deriving their authority from Plato: Poetry is useless and/or corrupting (somehow it's at once powerless and dangerous); it's less valuable than history or philosophy; in some important sense it's less real than other kinds of making. Sidney's famous and beautiful and confusing *The Defense of Poesy*—a work that helped establish the posture of poets and critics of poetry as essentially defensive—is the assertion of an ideal of imaginative literature more than an exaltation of actual poems. *Musica* Poetry, Sidney says in his wonderful *universalis* prose, is superior both to history and philosophy; it can move us, not just teach us facts; the poet is a creator who can transcend nature; thus poetry can

29

put us in touch with what's divine in us; and so on. But Sidney doesn't worry much about specific poems, which often suck: We shouldn't say "that poetry abuseth man's wit, but that man's wit abuseth poetry"—we shouldn't knock poetry because of bad poems. At the end of the defense, instead of supplying examples of great poems, Sidney just pities people who "cannot hear the planet-like music of poetry." (I, too, can't hear it.)

Even the most impassioned Romantic defenses of poetry reinscribe a sense of the insufficiency of poems. Shelley: "the most glorious poetry that has ever been communicated to the world is probably a feeble shadow of the original conception of the poet." A feeble shadow of an original conception sounds like Plato, although Plato didn't think a poet could really conceive of much. In Plato's time, poetry was dominant relative to the

new mode of philosophy he was attempting to advance; by the nineteenth
century, defenses of poetry must assert
the relevance of the art for a (novel-
reading) middle class preoccupied
with material things, what Shelley
calls the "excess of the selfish and cal-
culating principle." To defend poetry
as an alternative to material concerns
is both to continue and to invert the
Platonic critique. It is to accept the idea
that poems are less real—less truthful,
according to Plato—than other kinds
of representation, but to recast this
distance from material reality as a
virtuous alternative to our insatia-
ble hunger for money and things,
credit and cattle. This enables poets
and their defenders to celebrate poetic
capacity—"original conception"—over
and against the "feeble shadow" of real
poems.

Reading in my admittedly desultory
way across the centuries, I have come

to believe that a large part of the appeal of the defense as a genre is that it is itself a kind of virtual poetry—it allows you to describe the virtues of poetry without having to write poems that have succumbed to the bitterness *Replaced with* of the actual. Which is not to say that *slashes* defenses never cite specific poems, but lines of poetry quoted in prose preserve the glimmer of the unreal; to quote the narrator of my first novel who is here describing an exaggerated version of my own experience: "I tended to find lines of poetry beautiful only when I encountered them quoted in prose, in the essays my professors had assigned in college, where the line breaks were replaced with slashes, so that what was communicated was less a particular poem than the echo of poetic possibility."

The fatal problem with poetry: poems. This helps explain why poets themselves celebrate poets who

32

renounce writing. In college at the end of the last millennium the coolest young poets I knew were reading Rimbaud and Oppen—two very great and very different writers who had in common their abandonment of the art (although Oppen's was only temporary). Rimbaud stops writing at twenty or so and starts running guns; Oppen is famously silent for twenty-five years while he lives in Mexico to escape FBI inquiries into his labor organizing. Rimbaud is the enfant terrible who burns through the sayable; Oppen is the poet of the Left whose quiet is a sign of commitment. "Because I am not silent," Oppen wrote in a poem, "the poems are bad." Their silences as much as their works—or their silences as conceptual works—were what made them heroes to the aspiring poets I knew. It was as if writing were a stage we would pass through, as if poems were important because they could

33

be sacrificed on the altar of poetry in order to charge our silence with poetic virtuality. (And pretending to renounce poetry is everywhere within poems—quitting is a convention: You lament the insufficiency of your song, you destroy your oaten pipe. The fiction that a poem might be a poet's last bestows the promise of the virtual on the actual words. It's a technique at least as old as Virgil.) Thus the poet and the non-poet both ultimately achieve poemlessness, although the former passes through poems while the latter falls away from them.

I was reading Rimbaud on the green, careful to be seen, but I was also reading, savoring, the worst poets in English. One of the first books Keith and Rosmarie Waldrop—two of the most learned people I've ever met—gave me in Providence was an anthology their small press had published called *Pegasus Descending*, "A book of the best bad verse," a book that, as James Wright put it, contained "nothing mediocre!" This anthology *Φαιδων* of truly abysmal poems is, of course, often hilarious, but there's an element of idealism mixed into the hilarity: Reading the worst poems is a way of feeling, albeit negatively, that echo of poetic possibility. Think of Plato's argument in *Phaedo*, what's known as his "argument from imperfection": In order to perceive a particular thing to be imperfect, we must have in mind some ideal of perfection. If we perceive an apple to be an imperfect apple there must be a perfect Apple distinct from any particular apple. (Descartes, among others, will use a version of this to argue for the existence of God: I know I'm an imperfect being so I possess an idea of a perfect Being against which I'm measuring myself.) When we experience a poem's radical failure, we must be measuring it against some ideal, some Poem.

What if the closest we can come to hearing the "planet-like music of poetry" is to hear the ugliest earthly music and experience the distance between them? I remember the Waldrops would sometimes recite at their readings the work of William Topaz McGonagall, the nineteenth-century Scottish poet who Wikipedia contends has been "widely acclaimed as the worst poet in history" and whose "The Tay Bridge Disaster" is considered one of the most thoroughly horrible poems ever composed. In the winter of 1879, the Tay Bridge in the city of Dundee collapsed under a train, killing all passengers. McGonagall's poem (it's the second poem in a trilogy; the first poem praised the newly constructed bridge; the third poem praises its reconstruction) begins:

Beautiful railway bridge of the silv'ry
   Tay
Alas! I am very sorry to say
That ninety lives have been taken away
On the last sabbath day of 1879
Which will be remember'd for a very
   long time.

What I find compelling about this poem is how, when called upon to memorialize a faulty bridge, McGonagall constructs another one. The objective is to link the present of the disaster and the future, to create a community spanning time, but the technique fails spectacularly. Like any bad work of construction, the measurements are all wrong, its meter clumsy and irregular. It's clear McGonagall is earnestly trying to gather the resources of a metrical tradition, not subvert it, but the mismatch of duple and triple measure in the first line alone means that, while it's made of archival components

"The insufficiency of the cross bracing and its fastenings ...

(recognizable metrical feet), the line doesn't feel like it belongs to any specific metrical pattern (iambic, trochaic, dactylic, anapestic, etc.) or mode (pastoral, elegy, or ballad). I guess I read the first line as beginning with a dactyl (a stressed syllable followed by two unstressed syllables—BEAUtiful) and so I try to force "railway bridge" into the same stress pattern. But trying to read "bridge" as unstressed (especially given its thematic importance in the poem) feels weird, so then I revise my reading to recover the natural initial stress of RAILway and begin to divide the triple measure back into duple measure. This mishmash of meters (and of rising and falling rhythms) makes the ostensibly tactical elision of the third syllable from "silv'ry" preposterous. That gesture makes sense only as a way of carefully fitting "silvery" into a metrical framework that here doesn't exist.

The embarrassment of "silv'ry" can stand for how awful McGonagall is at integrating the tragedy into a tradition or the lost lives into a human community. There are a million ways to attack McGonagall's attempt at elegy, but crucial for me is how, just as he seems incapable of counting prosodic stresses, there is something disturbingly (and yet comically) off about his strategy for measuring lives and time. "I am very sorry to say" is a very sorry expression of sorrow, but perhaps more atrocious is the bland assignment of a number to the departed—an empty statistical abstraction, crass and calculative, exactly at the moment when I expect a poet to propound some alternative standard of value, or at least to indicate the felt desire to do so. (By the way, McGonagall was apparently wrong about the number of people who died: The death toll is now thought to have been seventy-five.)

... to sustain the force of the gale."

39

The mention of the "sabbath day" is presumably supposed to invoke the religious, to introduce the possibility of messianic time instead of mere clock time, but whatever hint of redemption the phrase carries is canceled by "1879," which here sounds as cold and abstract as "ninety." And because the numerically written year is an unscannable six-syllable mouthful, the end of the line is a prosodic train wreck. Rhyming "1879" with "time" itself—rhyming a mere number with the most general term for duration in the language—guarantees that the particular date the poem aspires to preserve vanishes into calendrical abstraction. What's so hilarious about the hurried "very long time" is that it sounds, after the disastrous description of the disaster, like a way of sheepishly hedging on the traditional claim of a poem to persist across generations. It's as if McGonagall might be saying:

This date could be remembered well into the 1890s. Or at least until 1883—and, after all, four years is a very long time! This horrible couplet is made worse by the fact that it's a refrain; it recurs three times in the poem.

And yet by hammering away at McGonagall's extreme failure here, I find myself implying a poem that could do something like the following: create a rhythm at once recognizably collective (because using the framework of inherited prosody) and irreducibly individual (because McGonagall's management of that framework would be expressive of his specific poetic voice), a rhythm that therefore enacts what the poem attempts to describe—the integration of individual (lost) lives into a human community that persists across time. I imply that there is some way to measure—in both the poetic and non-poetic sense of "measure"—lives and duration that resists the cold

Implied heights

exchangeability of the numerical and makes the past and present rhyme both literally and conceptually. My criticisms of McGonagall imply a poem that could transcend representation and defeat time. The demand I'm making of McGonagall is impossible.

I know it when I see it   I find it remarkable that his horribleness is evident even to those of us who don't read poetry. Recite this poem to a friend who has no interest in— or significant experience of—verse, who claims to know nothing about it, and I wager that she will concur, whether or not she can specify its failings, that it's at least very, *very* bad. In this way McGonagall succeeds by failing, because his failure can be recognized more or less universally and does in this sense produce community. "I know it when I see it," Justice Stewart famously said of hardcore pornography, and Louis Malle's *Les Amants*, which the state of Ohio was trying to ban, didn't qualify. It is much harder to agree on what constitutes a successful poem when we see it (we still respect Tolstoy, for instance, although he hated Shakespeare) than it is to agree that we're in the presence of an appalling one. I think that's because we feel the immense ambition—the impossible ambition—internal to a poem like McGonagall's, feel it all the more intensely because of the thoroughness with which his ambition outpaces his ability. A less bad poet would not make the distance between the virtual and the actual so palpable, so immediate. *Nothing mediocre*: The more abysmal the experience of the actual, the greater the implied heights of the virtual.

(I just got off the phone with my friend, the poet and critic Aaron Kunin —also a student, not coincidentally, of Grossman's—and mentioned my reading of "The Tay Bridge Disaster" only to be told by Kunin that Grossman obtained his job at Johns Hopkins by giving a talk on McGonagall and the Tay Bridge poems.)

A little more than fifty years before McGonagall wrote "The Tay Bridge Disaster" disaster, and about five hundred miles away from Dundee, John Keats was writing the six odes that many consider the closest thing we have in English to a realization of poetry's planet-like music. I won't offer up a bunch of examples of how fine Keats's ear is relative to McGonagall's (or, for that matter, anyone's), but I am struck by how even in Keats's most mellifluous odes, he describes an ideal music the poems themselves cannot make audible. From "Ode on a Grecian Urn":

> Heard melodies are sweet, but those
> unheard
> Are sweeter; therefore, ye soft pipes,
> play on;

Not to the sensual ear, but, more
   endear'd,
Pipe to the spirit ditties of no tone.

Many literary critics have discussed
the technical power of Keats's writing: how his poems suspend time or
create altered states in the reader, how
the music of his lines induces a trance.
I follow the literary critic Michael
Clune—also a student of Grossman—in
emphasizing how (1) for all my admiration for Keats, I can't experience the
trance these critics are talking about
(and also have some trouble believing   *Writ in water*
that they've experienced it, since I've
never seen any critic in a trancelike
state); and (2) at the heart of Keats's
poetry are what Clune calls "images
of a virtual music"—a music that Keats
can describe but not play (and that no-
body can play in time: It's not difficult,
it's impossible). Literary form cannot
actually produce the higher music

Keats imagines, it can only figure it, which is, in a sense, what McGonagall manages to do by being so bad. Keats's incredible skill, his woven vowels, tempt us into believing that the impossible music is just out of reach, whereas McGonagall's supreme ineptitude allows us to intuit its possibility via a confrontation with its opposite. Neither presents the genuine, and Keats, master that he is, doesn't even pretend to. I think of these lines from "Hyperion": "A living death was in each gush of sounds, / Each family of rapturous hurried notes, / That fell, one after one, yet all at once,"—those are gorgeous lines of ekphrastic verse, but what they describe cannot be realized by any human instrument in time.

Personally, I've never found Keatsian euphony quite as powerful as Emily Dickinson's dissonance. I think this is because Dickinson's distressed meters

and slant rhymes enable me to experience both extreme discord (although
in Dickinson it's eerie and controlled, *A flickering*
nothing like McGonagall) and a
virtuosic reaching for the music of the
spheres. I'll look at a poem to show
what I mean, but prior to considering
any particular example of Dickinson's
virtuality, it's worth noting that the
unusual nature of her manuscript
pages makes the status of a Dickinson
composition difficult to determine: Is
it a poem or some other kind of object?
A work of visual art? What about, for
instance, her "envelope writings"—
gently pried apart envelopes whose
physical shapes, some have argued, in-
teract purposefully with Dickinson's
language? Are her letters poems?
What about her notes on advertising
flyers? And those texts she gathered
into fascicles—hand-sewn groupings—
are full of variant words (which, as the
pioneering critic and poet Susan Howe

has argued, are part of the structure of the work, as are the crosses Dickinson uses to indicate them). Then there are the famous dashes, which I like to think of as, among other things, markers of the limits of the actual, vectors of implication where no words will do. For all the effort of (primarily male) editors to standardize Dickinson, her work, especially if seen in facsimile, throws a wrench in the bitter logic of the poetic principle by causing us to shift back and forth between modes of perception—we read one minute and look the next, the object refusing to become or to remain a typical poem. This is consistent with the emphasis across her work on the potential over the actual:

> I dwell in Possibility—
> A fairer House than Prose—
> More numerous of Windows—
> Superior—for Doors—

Of Chambers as the Cedars—
Impregnable of eye—
And for an everlasting Roof
The Gambrels of the Sky—

Of Visitors—the fairest—
For Occupation—This—
The spreading wide my narrow Hands
To gather Paradise—

Instead of the expected opposition of
poetry with prose, the former term is
replaced with "Possibility"—an im-
material dwelling, all threshold and
sky. The poem dramatizes the impossibility of actually gathering paradise;
the poetic occupation, the poem's
structure asserts, is spreading wide
the hands, not containing anything
within them (which is what it means
to dwell in the porous house of possibility). The poem goes out of its way
to emphasize the distance between the
short "i" of "This" and the long "i"

of "Paradise"—a rhyme the previous patterning would lead us to expect—and so we feel the distance between the writing of *this* poem on earth and whatever passes for Poetry in heaven. Long "i"'s are in every stanza of the house—the poem begins with one—and the sound of "eye" and "sky" is preserved in "wide," which, positioned above "Paradise" in both the manuscript and typed version, draws our attention to the parallelism of the two

terms, their vastness. But this can't compensate for the failure of "This" and "Paradise" to rhyme because meter and rhyme are in tension at the end of the poem, at least to my ear, which keeps "Paradise" from feeling like a true rhyme with "Sky." "Paradise" is normally dactylic (PARadise), but here the pressure to make it rhyme and scan requires promoting the final syllable (paraDISE, or PARaDISE). That's a common enough thing to do in a poem, to be sure, but Dickinson is so precise and weird that I find myself worrying over that alteration: I feel that I'm either stretching "Paradise," mangling it a little, in order to gather the rhyme, or letting the rhyme go in order to privilege pronunciation; I have to choose between "one after another"—the accentual unfolding of the word in time—or "all at once," the verticality of rhyme. All of this virtualizes the house the poem is, with a mixture of virtuosity and willed dissonance that captures something of both Keats's music and McGonagall's collapsing bridge.

McGonagall, Keats, Dickinson— they make a place for the genuine by producing a negative image of the ideal Poem we cannot write in time. The horrible and the great (and the silent) have more in common than the mediocre, or OK, or even pretty good, because they rage against the merely

Via negativa

actual, have a perfect contempt for it (or, in the case of the painfully earnest McGonagall, at least readily inspire such contempt), in order to approach on a *via negativa* the imaginary work that could reconcile the finite and the infinite, the individual and the communal, which can make a new world out of the linguistic materials of this one. *I, too, dislike it*: That "too" in the Moore is important—poet and reader of poetry are united in a suspicion of the song of any "earthly poet," and that suspicion is the ground for an intuition of the ideal. The hatred of poetry is internal to the art, because it is the task of the poet and poetry reader to use the heat of that hatred to burn the actual off the virtual like fog.

Great poets as different as Keats and Dickinson express their contempt for merely actual poems by developing techniques for virtualizing their own compositions—by dissolving the actual poem into an image of the Poem literary form cannot achieve. But there is an important class of intense poetry haters who would probably hate my description of poetry as providing a kind of inverted and necessarily limited glimmer of poetic potentiality: the avant-garde. "Avant-garde" was originally a (French) military term for those elite soldiers who were dispatched ahead of the rest of an armed force in order to determine its course. The first recorded use of the term in its more or less contemporary artistic sense was in a 1596 work by the historian Étienne Pasquier: "A glorious war was then being waged against ignorance, a war whose avant-garde was constituted by [three poets you've never heard of]; or, to put it another way, these men were the forerunners of the other poets." And the sense of the "avant-garde" as a group of artists capable of revolutionizing not only the word but also the world is at least as old as an 1825 essay by the social reformer Olinde Rodrigues, who claimed artists function as the people's avant-garde because "the power of the arts is ... the most immediate and fastest way" to achieve sociopolitical reform. The idea that poems (or other artworks) can intervene directly in history is crucial here. In his influential *Theory of the Avant-Garde*, the German critic Peter Bürger claimed that what defines the historical avant-garde is a desire to destroy the institution of art and instead make it part of the "praxis of life"—to abolish art as a separate category from the rest of our experience. For the avant-garde, the poem is an imaginary bomb with real shrapnel: It explodes the category of poetry and enters history. The poem is a weapon— a weapon against received ideas of what the artwork is, certainly, but also an instrument of war in a heroic,

An instrument of war

54

revolutionary struggle, whether of the far Right (e.g., the Italian Futurists) or the far Left (e.g., the Russian Futurists).

There have been, of course, and continue to be multiple self-declared avant-gardes, and any generalization is necessarily reductive—often the term is just used to describe formally experimental work—but for our purposes we can say: The avant-garde hates poems. It hates existing poems because they are part of a bankrupt society—literature has "magnified pensive immobility, ecstasy and slumber. We want to exalt movements of aggression, feverish sleeplessness, the double march, the perilous leap, the slap and the blow with the fist." Thus the Italian Futurists, often considered the first important vanguard movement. Life is a lie and poems have been the flower of that lie and they function to glorify or compensate for existing relations that must be destroyed.

This hatred of existing poetry gives rise to the avant-garde poem in which formal experiment is going to eviscerate existing canons of taste and help bring about the revolution. So Marinetti, to stay with the Italians, advocates a language that's broken free of syntax ("*Parole in Libertà*") and that experiments with typography ("*Immaginazione Senza Fili*"; "*Analogia Disegnata*") and pure sound (cf. "*Zang Tumb Tumb*"), and these works obliterate what passed for culture in the past, obliterate the category of art itself. (I note in passing that Marinetti's "The Manifesto of Futurism" is read much more widely than any of his actual poems; the genre of the manifesto, like the defense, allows you to make claims for and about Poetry while avoiding the limitations of poems.) The problem is that these artworks, no matter how formally inventive, remain artworks. They might redefine the borders of art, but they don't erase those borders; a bomb that never goes off, the poem remains a poem. And they hate that. The avant-garde is a military metaphor that forgets it is a metaphor. The Futurists—ghosts of the future past—enter the museums they wanted to flood.

I'm offering this aggressively cursory summary of avant-garde hatred—a particularly bitter poetic logic—because I think it gets at something crucial about the disdain for poetry. Even writers and critics allergic to anything resembling avant-garde rhetoric often express anger at poetry's failure to achieve any real political effects, an anger that perhaps dates back to Plato's flattering insistence that poets are dangerous to the Republic. The avant-garde imagines itself as hailing from the future it wants to bring about, but many people express disappointment in poetry for failing

to live up to the political power it supposedly possessed in the past. This
disappointment in the political feeble-
ness of poetry in the present unites
Nostalgia for the futurist and the nostalgist and is a
the future staple of mainstream denunciations of
poetry.

Here's just one example of what
I mean. When Barack Obama an-
nounced that he would revive the
practice of having a poem read at his
2009 Inauguration—Clinton had done
it twice; Kennedy had done it in 1961—
George Packer wondered on the *New
Yorker* blog: "Is it too late to con-
vince the President-elect not to have
a poem written for and read at his
Inauguration?" He explained:

> For many decades American poetry
> has been a private activity, written by
> few people and read by few people,
> lacking the language, rhythm, emotion,
> and thought that could move large

58

numbers of people in large public settings.

I find the ambiguity of "for many decades" telling; was there a poet in, say, the fifties who could have—through the power of his or her "language, rhythm, emotion, and thought"— moved a diverse crowd assembled on the Mall? Or is Packer longing for MLK's oratory, in which case why *Is it too late* pick on poetry? And does "move" here just mean move emotionally, or does it mean move to something— a greater sense of civic identity or responsibility, a specific action? While Packer suggests that Derek Walcott "might have pulled it off" (how, I'm not sure) he's dubious about Elizabeth Alexander, whom Obama selected to compose the poem. Packer, having taken a look at Alexander's website, says:

Alexander writes with a fine, angry

irony, in vividly concrete images, but her poems have the qualities of most contemporary American poetry—a specificity that's personal and unsuggestive, with moves toward the general that are selfconsciously academic. They are not poems that would read well before an audience of millions.

The problem with Alexander, as with most American poets, is that she's too specific and too general—and where she's general she's selfconscious about generality (perhaps like many of us she shares some hesitation about her right to speak for *everyone*, and Packer, in a familiar move, blames her lack of universality on her time in the university). As with my attack on McGonagall, Packer's criticisms suggest, albeit negatively, a poetic ideal—a poet who could unite us in our difference, constituting a collective subject through the magic of language and prosody, one who, by speaking for herself, could speak for every self: an I that contains multitudes. And such a poem, Packer implies, would cease being poetry and enter history. Unlike the avant-garde fantasy of an elite that pulls us into the future, however, Packer projects this unifying bard into the past. Instead of the formal difficulty of an avant-garde— a difficulty intended to scandalize and short-circuit bourgeois sensibility in the service of a revolutionary project—Packer mourns the lost unifying power that poetry supposedly formerly had. He doesn't have to do much more than glance at a website to realize Alexander isn't up to the task: She is, after all, writing actual poems.

"I am large, I contain multitudes," Walt Whitman wrote in "Song of Myself," and Packer's nostalgia, as with many American nostalgists, is clearly shaped by the figure of

A bard projected into the past

61

Whitman, who desired his book, *Leaves of Grass*, to be a kind of secular bible for American democracy. The American experiment—its newness, its geographical vastness, the relative openness of its institutions, its egalitarianism, its orientation toward the future and not the past—all of these necessitated, in Whitman's view, an equally new and expansive poetry: plainspoken, unrestrained by inherited verse structures, just as the country would be unrestrained by monarchic traditions, and so on. "There will soon be no more priests," Whitman wrote, "their work is done." What was needed was a poet who, in the absence of a common tradition or metaphysical system, could celebrate the American people into existence, who could help hold the nation together, in all its internal difference, through his singing. From his "Song of the Exposition":

A bard projected into the future

Thou Union holding all, fusing,
    absorbing, tolerating all,
Thee, ever thee, I sing.

Thou, also thou, a World,
With all thy wide geographies,
    manifold, different, distant,
Rounded by thee in one—one common
    orbic language,
One common indivisible destiny
    for All.

Whitman's search for a poetic correlative to an idealized American political project is reflected in (at least) two formal characteristics of his work: the length and inclusiveness of his lines and the capaciousness of his pronouns. Whitman's famous catalogues—his long lists—model federalism in their very structure, uniting in a single extended syntactic unit all the differences (of people's class, race, gender, geography, etc.) that threaten the

Orbic language

coherence of "the people"; his lines are always trying to "hold all," always unenjambed. In fact, the unconventional extension and lack of traditional verse patterning of Whitman's lines makes them approach prose, as if Whitman, in pursuing his poetic ideal for the United States, was getting rid of actual poems—replacing them with something more like journalism or oratory. (Perhaps we can think of this as Whitman's tactic for virtualizing poetry just as Dickinson's strange texts always threaten to be something other than poems. Moreover, no page can contain Whitman's lines; they are always running over the right margin, and so must be continued and indented on the next line to show that the break is a result of the objective limitations of space, not a poet's individual decision. I like to think of this "orphaning" of lines as another form of virtualization: The union toward which the long lines gesture cannot be actualized in any book, at least any book of standard size.)

Whitman democratizes pronouns in order to attempt to make room for any reader in his "I" and "you," so that a celebration of the former is also a celebration of the latter, as in three of the most famous lines in American poetry, the opening of "Song of Myself": "I celebrate myself, and sing myself, / And what I assume you shall assume, / For every atom belonging to me as good belongs to you." In many ways "Walt Whitman" is less a historical person than a kind of placeholder for democratic personhood. In the 1855 edition of *Leaves of Grass*, "Walt Whitman" doesn't appear on the title page. It's only in "Song of Myself" that the reader encounters the author's name: "Walt Whitman, an American, one of the rough, a kosmos." The effect is to signal that

"Walt Whitman" is an enabling fiction produced by the poems themselves— a figure with whom readers can identify, whether in 1855 or in the future. And Whitman in fact divulges very little personal information, particulars that might get in the way of our ability to exchange atoms. We hear almost nothing about the contingencies of his experience; if his individuality were too differentiated, we wouldn't find ourselves exchangeable. Instead, Whitman's "I" is comprised of a series of general contradictions ("Do I contradict myself? / Very well then I contradict myself"). He is (or supposes himself to be) the poet of man and woman, the poet of good and the poet of wickedness, asserting the humanity both of the master and the slave, etc. And the things he sees and enumerates in his poems are things that pretty much anybody might see. In "Crossing Brooklyn Ferry," one of his

Who includes diversity and is nature

66

many explicit addresses to the future, he notes light in the water, some ships, buildings, flags—particulars general enough to be almost anyone's perceptions. "[A] hundred years hence, or ever so many hundred years hence, others will see them." Walt Whitman is himself a *place* for the genuine, an open space or textual commons where American readers of the future can forge and renew their sense of possibility and interconnectedness. No doubt part of why Whitman addressed himself relentlessly to the future was so his actual historical person—the Walt Whitman of the title page—would be dead and gone, freeing him to function as a kind of messianic figure within the poems.

A man without qualities

But the Whitmanic program has never been realized in history, and I don't think it can be: Whitman comes to stand for the contradictions of a democratic personhood that cannot become actual without becoming exclusive. To quote Grossman's brilliant essay on Whitman—as I write this monograph I come to realize with greater and greater clarity how central Grossman's thinking is for me—Whitman announces "the presence of the person prior to all other characteristics." You don't need me to tell you that Whitman's dreamed union has never arrived, but I believe his vision nevertheless determines Packer's Inaugural nostalgia for a poetry that could supposedly reconcile the individual and *E pluribus* the social, and so transform millions *unum* of individuals into an authentic People. Whitman deferred poetic realization into the future ("I stop somewhere, waiting for you"), but many poetry haters act as though the project was realized at some unspecifiable moment in the past and then undone as the art and/or its public declined. This allows them to repudiate poems in the present while reasserting a Whitmanic belief in the power of poetry (if also thereby betraying Whitman's belief in future perfectability over any longing for the past).

One thing I've always found fascinating about Whitman is his claim that, on the one hand, he's doing the most important work that can be done, producing a technology for the formation and perpetual renewal of the greatest people on the planet, and, on the other hand, that he's doing no work at all: He's always "loafing," taking his ease. Whitman has tremendous admiration for American workers of all sorts (see, for instance, "I Hear America Singing"), but he doesn't want to be one; he appears to think leisure is a condition of poetic receptivity. "I loafe and invite my soul, / I lean and loafe at my ease observing a spear of summer grass." I think part of this has to do with the question of emptying himself out: If Whitman were a shoe-maker or hatter, he would sing only *At my ease* the song of shoemakers or hatters respectively ("The shoemaker sing-ing as he sits on his bench, the hatter singing as he stands"), instead of being able to sing about work in the abstract ("Each singing what belongs to him or her and to none else"). Whitman can sing difference but cannot differentiate himself without compromising his labor—which is part of why his labor has to be a kind of leisure, a profes-sion that transcends the professions; Whitman can't take sides. In this re-gard his work as a Civil War nurse seems significant: He can tend the sick, recognize the humanity of the soldiers (from the North, but also the South), and love these historical per-sons as they are sacrificed for the future union. But he cannot fight.

The question of whether poetry is work or leisure (or somehow both or

70

neither) is everywhere in denunciations and defenses of the art. Sidney suggested that the poet did a kind of higher work than others because he produced ideal images of sovereigns—the job of the poet isn't to work at court but to suggest that toward which a court might aspire. For Romantics like Shelley, poetry checks the "calculative" avarice of a materialistic society, offering an alternative to a crass utilitarianism that is blind to everything that can't be instrumentalized; the use of poetry is therefore entwined with its uselessness. (Shelley was responding to Thomas Love Peacock's argument in "The Four Ages of Poetry" that science had rightfully supplanted poetry as civilization had advanced.) It's precisely because of the contradictory nature of the poetic vocation—it is both more and less than work, its usefulness depends on its lack of practical utility—that we are embarrassed by

Get a real job

71

and disdainful of the poet's labor.

"Poetry" is supposed to signify an alternative to the kind of value that circulates in the economy as we live it daily, but actual poems can't realize that alternative. This is why telling a poet to "get a real job," a familiar injunction from poetry haters, is in fact a powerful and traditional command: Do actual work instead of virtual work for once. (This is related to how poets and non-poets both tend to attack poets for entering the academy, for becoming teachers: On the one hand, it's too mercenary, too close to a real job—you get paid, you have an office [if you're lucky]; on the other hand, it repeats the scandal of leisure—the academy isn't the "real world," you don't work "real" hours, it's impossible to measure whether you're transmitting skills, and so on. A poet in the academy is resented for being at once too actual and too virtual in her labor.) "Poetry"

is a word for a kind of value no particular poem can realize: the value of
persons, the value of a human activity
beyond the labor/leisure divide, a value before or beyond price. Thus hating
poems can either be a way of negatively
expressing poetry as an ideal—a way of
expressing our desire to exercise such
imaginative capacities, to reconstitute
the social world—or it can be a defensive rage against the mere suggestion
that another world, another measure
of value, is possible. In the latter case,
the hatred of poetry is a kind of reac-
tion formation: You lash out against
the symbol of what you're repressing,
i.e., creativity, community, a desire for
a measure of value that isn't "calculative." "Poetry" becomes a word for an
outside that poems cannot bring about,
but can make felt, albeit as an absence, *The death of*
albeit through embarrassment. The pe- *poetry*
riodic denunciations of contemporary
poetry should therefore be understood

as part of the bitter logic of poetry, not as its repudiation. This is why so many cultural critics, with a kind of macabre glee, proclaim "the death of poetry" every few years: Our imaginative faculties, we fear, have atrophied; the commercialization of language seems complete. The actual number of poems being written and read appears to be irrelevant to the certification of poetry's death—a decade ago, James Longenbach reported there were more than three hundred thousand websites devoted to poetry—because what the pronouncement reflects is less an empirical statement about poems than a cultural anxiety about our capacity for "alternative making."

Many of the periodic essays worrying over the state of American poetry have, despite their avowed democratic aspirations, an implicit politics that makes me uneasy. Consider one of the most recent high-profile jeremiads,

Mark Edmundson's "Poetry Slam: Or, The decline of American verse," which appeared in the July 2013 issue of *Harper's Magazine*. Edmundson's essay contends that contemporary poets, while talented, have ceased to be politically ambitious. The primary problem is that, while many poems are "good in their ways," they "simply aren't good enough"; this is because "They don't slake a reader's thirst for meanings that pass beyond the experience of the individual poet and light up the world we hold in common." Once again, the problem with poets is their failure to be universal, to speak both to and for everyone in the manner of Whitman, who Edmundson, of course, evokes. (Why Whitman should be considered a success and not a failure is never addressed; again, it's as if Whitman's dream was realized in some vague past the nostalgists can never quite pinpoint.)

Light up the world

Edmundson makes a few silly claims, e.g., that contemporary writers haven't responded to the influence or language of popular culture (maybe he didn't read any of the Ashbery he criticizes?), or that the poets he singles out—mainstream, celebrated poets such as Jorie Graham and Frank Bidart—have never attempted to take on issues of national significance. Whatever you think of these poets, these claims are merely false. Putting that aside, according to Edmundson, the problem with contemporary poets is that they're concerned with the individual voice:

Contemporary American poets now seem to put all their energy into one task: the creation of a voice. They strive to sound like no one else. And that often means poets end up pushing what is most singular and idiosyncratic in themselves and in the language to

the fore and ignoring what they have
in common with others.

Seamus Heaney is criticized for
sounding like Seamus Heaney and not
everyone else; "John Ashbery sounds
emphatically like John Ashbery"; etc.
These tautologies echo Packer's (and
many others') concerns: Individuals
are too individual to speak for everyone. Who is at fault? The university,
because the university has taught us
to be, to recall Packer's term, "selfconscious" about generalizations:

> How dare a white female poet say "we"
> and so presume to speak for her black
> and brown contemporaries? How dare
> a white male poet speak for anyone
> but himself? And even then, given
> the crimes and misdemeanors his sort
> have visited, how can he raise his voice
> above a self-subverting whisper?

Well, how dare he or she? Edmundson raises these questions as if it were obviously PC cowardice not to claim the right to speak for everyone. But then, his essay strongly suggests that he considers speaking for everyone the exclusive domain of white men. He praises Sylvia Plath, for instance, but note how her work—singled out as an example of the ambitious writing we currently lack—turns out only to speak for women:

White male nostalgia

> Sylvia Plath may or may not overtop the bounds of taste and transgress the limits of metaphor when she compares her genteel professor father to a Nazi brute. ("Every woman adores a Fascist.") But she challenges all women to reimagine the relations between fathers and daughters.

Edmundson apparently cannot imagine a father reading the poem and feeling challenged. When Robert Lowell writes, however, he is "calling things as he believed them to be not only for himself but for all of his readers." Somehow, according to Edmundson, "Waking Early Sunday Morning"—one of Lowell's most famous antiwar poems—speaks for everyone: "Lowell speaks directly of *our* children, *our* monotonous sublime: few are the consequential poets now who are willing to venture that 'our.'" Plath helps daughters reimagine their relationships with their fathers; Lowell is everybody's father. Lowell's specific cultural allusions—the title echoes Stevens, the prosodic structure recalls Marvell—apparently make him universal (Whitman, by the way, would have rejected these techniques as too exclusive and staid for the American experiment).

The weirdest moment in the essay might be when Edmundson, probably

That *our*

eager to give an example of a nonwhite person who can speak for the collective, discusses what he calls Amiri Baraka's "consequential and energetic political poem," "Somebody Blew Up America." The poem received widespread attention because Baraka—who was then the poet laureate of New Jersey—included the following quatrain:

> Who knew the World Trade Center
>   was gonna get bombed
> Who told 4000 Israeli workers at the
>   Twin Towers
> To stay home that day
> Why did Sharon stay away?

The poem was "consequential" in the sense that it caused New Jersey to dissolve the position of poet laureate—Baraka refused to resign and it turned out there was no constitutional mechanism for his removal—and the poem earned a place in the Anti-Defamation League archive. I can imagine cogent arguments praising or excusing or bashing Baraka's poem, but I am startled by Edmundson's claim that this poem is at least "an attempt to say not how it is for Baraka exclusively but how it is for all." It's true that Baraka's poem is not concerned with the particulars of his individual experience, but it is not at all true that the poem isn't unmistakably in Baraka's voice; regardless, how do lines like the following speak for "all"?

They say it's some terrorist,
some barbaric
A Rab,
in Afghanistan
It wasn't our American terrorists
It wasn't the Klan or the Skin heads
Or the them that blows up nigger
Churches, or reincarnates us on
  Death Row

It wasn't Trent Lott
Or David Duke or Giuliani
Or Schundler, Helms retiring

Most of the poem is devoted to cata-
loging the violence done to people
of color by white Americans. Since
Edmundson evokes Baraka's inten-
tions, we might as well quote Baraka's
account of his own poem:

> The poem's underlying theme focuses
> on how Black Americans have suffered
> from domestic terrorism since being
> kidnapped into U.S. chattel slavery,
> e.g., by Slave Owners, U.S. & State
> Laws, Klan, Skin Heads, Domestic
> Nazis, Lynching, denial of rights, na-
> tional oppression, racism, character
> assassination, historically, and at this
> very minute throughout the U.S. The
> relevance of this to Bush's call for
> a "War on Terrorism," is that Black
> people feel we have always been vic-
> tims of terror, governmental and

82

general, so we cannot get as frenzied and hysterical as the people who [ask us] to dismiss our history and contemporary reality to join them, in the name of a shallow "patriotism" in attacking the majority of people in the world, especially people of color and in the third world.

The "we" here is purposefully not "all"; indeed, Baraka's point is explicitly to refuse the false "we" politicians are attempting to deploy—a "we" that tactically forgets the history of anti-Black violence as it attempts to constitute a unified front in the "War on Terror," which in turn involves killing more people of color. To suggest that Baraka's "we" is an attempt to speak for "all" is therefore to repeat the dismissal of "our [people of color's] history and contemporary reality."

I can forgive Edmundson for his bad examples only in the sense that

At this very minute (Eric Garner, Mike Brown, Eric Harris, Freddie Gray, Tamir Rice, Akai Gurley, Laquan McDonald...)

there are no *good* examples of "superb lyric poems" that at once "have something to say" utterly specific to a poet's "experience" and can speak for all. (Edmundson might say what he demands is that a poet attempt that impossible task and fail, but his readings lead us to suspect he believes that white men will fail better.) The lyric—that is, the intensely subjective, personal poem—that can authentically encompass everyone is an impossibility in a world characterized by difference and violence. This is not to indict the desire for such a poem (indeed, the word we often use for such desire is "Poetry") but to indict the celebration of any specific poem for having achieved this unreachable goal because that necessarily involves passing off particularity as universality. Edmundson lacks a perfect contempt for the actual examples he considers; he confuses the Poem you sing in the dream with the poem you sing by the fire.

The capacity to transcend history has historically been ascribed to white men of a certain class while *Fail better* denied to individuals marked by difference (whether of race or gender). Edmundson's (jokey?) acknowledgment of the "crimes and misdemeanors" white men have committed in their effort to speak as if they were everyone can hardly count as an engagement with—let alone a refutation of—this inequality. As Claudia Rankine and Beth Loffreda put it in a recent essay:

> What we want to avoid at all costs is ... an opposition between writing that accounts for race ... and writing that is "universal." If we continue to think of the "universal" as better-than, as the pinnacle, we will always discount writing that doesn't look universal because it accounts for race or some other demeaned category. The universal is

85

a fantasy. But we are captive, still, to a sensibility that champions the universal while simultaneously defining the universal, still, as white. We are captive, still, to a style of championing literature that says work by writers of color succeeds when a white person can nevertheless relate to it—that it "transcends" its category.

What makes Whitman so powerful and powerfully embarrassing is that he is explicit about the contradictions inherent in the effort to "inhabit all." This is also what makes it so silly to imply Whitman's poetic ideal was ever accomplished in the past and that we've since declined—because of identity politics—into avoidable fractiousness. "I am the poet of the slaves, and of the masters of slaves," Whitman wrote in his journal, indicating the impossible desire to both recognize and suspend difference within his poems, to be no

And of the masters

86

one in particular so he could stand for everyone. You can hate contemporary poetry—in any era—as much as you want for failing to realize the fantasy of universality, but the haters should stop pretending any poem ever successfully spoke for everyone.

Claudia Rankine's own writing reflects many of the contradictory political demands made of poetry while providing a contemporary example of how a poet might strategically explore the limits of the actual. Rankine's last two books—*Don't Let Me Be Lonely: An American Lyric* and *Citizen: An American Lyric*—announce in their common subtitles a tension between a national project and a personal one. More specifically, Rankine confronts—as an African-American woman—the impossibility (and impossible complexity) of attempting to reconcile herself with a racist society in which to be black is either to be invisible

Trauma counseling

87

(excluded from the universal) or all too visible (as the victim of racist surveillance and aggression). The invitation to read these two volumes as lyric poetry strains against one of their most notable formal features: The books are mainly written in prose. And that prose is "measured" less in the sense of having a poetic prosody than in the sense of evincing a kind of restraint, verging on flatness, exhaustion, dissociation. I'll quote at some length from *Don't Let Me Be Lonely* to give a sense of the tone:

> Or one begins asking oneself that same question differently. Am I dead? Though this question at no time explicitly translates into Should I be dead, eventually the suicide hotline is called. You are, as usual, watching television, the eight-o'clock movie, when a number flashes on the screen: I-800-SUICIDE. You dial the number. Do you feel like

killing yourself? the man on the other end of the receiver asks. You tell him, I feel like I am already dead. When he makes no response you add, I am in death's position. He finally says, Don't believe what you are thinking and feeling. Then he asks, Where do you live?

Fifteen minutes later the doorbell rings. You explain to the ambulance attendant that you had a momentary lapse of happily. The noun, happiness, is a static state of some Platonic ideal you know better than to pursue. Your modifying process had happily or unhappily experienced a momentary pause. This kind of thing happens, perhaps is still happening. He shrugs and in turn explains that you need to come quietly or he will have to restrain you. If he is forced to restrain you, he will have to report that he is forced to restrain you. It is this simple: Resistance will only make matters more difficult. Any resistance will only make matters worse. By law,

I will have to restrain you. His tone suggests that you should try to understand the difficulty in which he finds himself. This is further disorienting. I am fine! Can't you see that! You climb into the ambulance unassisted.

The "lyric" is traditionally associated with brevity, intensely felt emotion, and highly musical verse; Rankine's writing here is purposely none of those things; to claim it as lyric would baffle Keats. Rankine's work is extremely personal, but primarily in the sense that she frankly explores the experience of depersonalization—numbness, desensitization, media saturation (and what passes for a social response to those things: a hotline, mandated restraint, etc.). What I encounter in Rankine is the felt unavailability of traditional lyric categories; the instruction to read her writing as poetry—and especially as lyric poetry—catalyzes an experience of their loss, like a sensation in a phantom limb. (The effect would be muffled if not altogether absent if the work was presented as an essay and not as a poem.) "Do feelings lose their feeling if they speak to a lack of feeling?" Rankine asks at one point in *Citizen*. I think her work answers that question in the negative by making us feel a desire for feeling beyond stereotype and spectacle. "Poetry" becomes a word for that possibility whose absence we sense in these poems— except, perhaps, in those instances where Rankine quotes other poems within the body of her text, something she does frequently in *Don't Let Me Be Lonely*. There, the poems have the glimmer of the virtual by virtue of their appearance within the frame of Rankine's prose: I read the cited poem not merely as itself but as a touchstone or talisman for Rankine in her effort

"I am already dead"

91

to create, on however small a scale, a "we" through poetic citation that can rouse her out of "death's position."

Let me quote a page from *Citizen* to further show how Rankine's work virtualizes the poem to powerful effect:

The new therapist specializes in trauma counseling. You have only ever spoken to her on the phone. Her house has a side gate that leads to a back entrance she uses for patients. You walk down a path bordered on both sides with deer grass and rosemary to the gate, which turns out to be locked.

At the front door the bell is a small round disc that you press firmly. When the door finally opens, the woman standing there yells, at the top of her lungs, Get away from my house! What are you doing in my yard?

It's as if a wounded Doberman pinscher or a German shepherd has gained the power of speech. And though you back up a few steps, you manage to tell her you have an appointment. You have an appointment? she spits back. Then she pauses. Everything pauses. Oh, she says, followed by, oh, yes, that's right. I am sorry.

I am so sorry, so, so sorry.

The play of pronouns in *Citizen* is discomfiting and a compelling refutation of the nostalgist fantasies of universality discussed above. Here the "you" is presumably Rankine, but of course I am, as I read, the recipient of the address. This is uncomfortable initially simply because of what's happening to the "you"—the ferocious response of the therapist to "my" presence. But I also then quickly, if after a pause, reject my identification with the "you" because I am aware of how I, a white man, cannot in fact relate to the experience in question; I cannot be a victim of such racism; I am in that regard much closer to the "I." My unease in momentarily misidentifying with the victim is, of course, hardly commensurate with the misidentification of which Rankine is the actual victim ("you," because black, are a trespasser). My privilege excludes me—that is, protects me—from the "you" in a way that focuses my attention on the much graver (and mundane) exclusion of a person of color from the "you" that the scene recounts (how could *you* have an appointment). *Citizen*'s concern with how race determines when and how we have access to pronouns is, among many other things, a direct response to the Whitmanic (and nostalgist) notion of a perfectly exchangeable "I" and "you" that can suspend all difference. Whoever you are, while reading *Citizen*, you are forced to situate yourself relative to the pronouns

94

as opposed to assuming you fit within them. There is both critique and desire here—a confrontation with false universality and a testing of the possibilities of a second person that won't let me, whoever I am, be lonely: "to call you out, to call out you."

In the excerpts of *Citizen* that appeared in magazines and in the prepublication galleys circulated to reviewers, Rankine's poems were often preceded by, followed by, or broken up by slashes. The " / "—the technical term is "virgule"—is the conventional way of indicating a line break when verse is quoted in prose. I think it's notable that the virgule often appeared after or between prose passages in *Citizen* where it could be read as a typographical representation of verse's felt unavailability—or, to put it another way, verse's ghostly presence. I called Dickinson's dash a vector of implication, a way of gesturing toward what language can't contain, and in that sense a signature of the virtual; in the first versions of *Citizen* I encountered, the virgules lurked around the texts like a sign of banished possibility. (There are other virtualizing techniques in *Citizen*; for example, part of the book consists of "scripts" made for videos by John Lucas; encountering the script, but not the moving image, we read the texts as notes for a performance the book does not, cannot, actually present.) The virgule is the irreducible mark of poetic virtuality—the line break abstracted from the time and space of an actual poem. Rankine removed the " / " in the final version of *Citizen*, as if to indicate a shift from the more virtual space of the excerpt or galley to the "final" form of the book. Because I think Rankine's work depends on making the lyric felt as a loss, I personally wish she'd left the virgules in.

Virgula Divina

Rankine isn't the only poet to use the " / ." Indeed, the virgule has a quiet but, I think, important presence in American poetry of the last half a century or so. The first poem in Donald Allen's *The New American Poetry, 1945–1960*, an inestimably influential anthology for several generations of poets, is Charles Olson's "The Kingfishers," a poem that for many, and in many ways, marks the threshold of postwar American poetry. It's a poem whose title and central figure evoke and invert a major motif in T. S. Eliot's *The Waste Land* (the Fisher King), and whose enjambment, assemblage, and attempt to gather a live tradition from diverse materials is obviously indebted to Ezra Pound's *Cantos*. And yet, in its refusal of modernist nostalgia for some lost unity of experience and its rejection of totalizing ideologies, it seeks to re-cover poetic experiment from the

97

catastrophes of modernity. This is its famous first line:

What does not change / is the will to
change

I'm not sure if this is one line of poetry, or two lines, or zero—that is, is it one line of actual verse, or is it two lines of verse presented as citation? The slash exists in Pound; Olson is copying it from the *Pisan Cantos* ("That maggots shd / eat the dead Bullock"), and Pound is copying it, according to Guy Davenport, from John Adams's letters, where such abbreviations were common. So the virgule itself is being quoted, another level of virtuality. My point is that here, at what for many constitutes the beginning of postwar American poetry, we don't exactly have a poem at all: We have something that can be read and cannot not be read on some level—especially coming from a poet who was a critic first—as a citation or example of verse. Despite Olson's emphasis in his essays on the technical achievements of "open field poetry," I think his famous first line is a way of announcing that his poem is a virtual space, not yet or not just an actual poem. ("I tended to find lines of poetry beautiful only when I encountered them quoted in prose ... so that what was communicated was less a particular poem ...")

"Virgule": from Latin *virgula*—a little rod, from *virga*: branch, rod. We hear in it the *Virgula Divina*—the divining rod that locates water or other precious substances underground, a rod that mediates or pretends to mediate between the terrestrial and the divine. We hear (although the etymology is disputed) the name of the ancient poet known to us as Virgil, Dante's guide through hell. And we hear the meteorological phenomenon known as "virga," my favorite kind of weather: streaks of water or ice particles trailing from a cloud that evaporate before they reach the ground. It's a rainfall that never quite closes the gap between heaven and earth, between the dream and fire; it's a mark for verse that is not yet, or no longer, or not merely actual; they are phenomena whose failure to become or remain fully real allows them to figure something beyond the phenomenal.

Like rain that never reaches ground

Great poets confront the limits of actual poems, tactically defeat or at least suspend that actuality, sometimes quit writing altogether, becoming celebrated for their silence; truly horrible poets unwittingly provide a glimmer of virtual possibility via the extremity of their failure; avant-garde poets hate poems for remaining poems instead of becoming bombs; and nostalgists hate poems for failing to do what they wrongly, vaguely claim poetry once

100

did. There are varieties of interpene-trating demands subsumed under the word "poetry"—to defeat time, to still it beautifully; to express irreducible individuality in a way that can be recognized socially or, à la Whitman, to achieve universality by being irre-ducibly social, less a person than a national technology; to defeat the lan-guage and value of existing society; to propound a measure of value beyond money. But one thing all these de-mands share is that they can't ever be fulfilled with poems. Hating on actual poems, then, is often an ironic if sometimes unwitting way of express-ing the persistence of the utopian ideal of Poetry, and the jeremiads in that regard are defenses, too.

The persistent demand

I hope it goes without saying that my summary here doesn't pretend to be comprehensive—poems can fulfill any number of ambitions other than the ones I'm describing. They can *actually* be funny, or lovely, or offer solace, or courage, or inspiration to certain audiences at certain times; they can play a role in constituting a community; and so on. The admitted weakness in the story I'm telling about Poetry is that it doesn't have much to say about good poems in all their variety; it's much better at dealing with great or horrible instances of the art. (And I don't pretend to know where the art begins or ends: Another essay might look at how hip-hop, or spoken word, or other creative linguistic practices take up "/" or bypass the contradictions I've been describing.) But the story is illuminating because it helps account for the persistent if mutable feeling that our moment's poems are always already failing us—whether our moment is 380 BC or 731, or 1579, or 1819, or 2016. If the poems are impenetrable, they are elitist, only allowing some brainy elect into the community of persons because, as we all sense, a person is someone who can find consciousness shareable through poetry; if they are clichéd, they embarrass us badly, showing internality to be only communicable through language that's been deadened, depersonalized by its popularity; and if they are weapons in a revolutionary struggle, they seem only to shoot blanks. Poets are liars not because, as Socrates says, they can fool us with the power of their imitations, but because identifying yourself as a poet implies you might overcome the bitter logic of the poetic principle, and you can't. You can only compose poems that, when read with perfect contempt, clear a place for the genuine Poem that never appears.

—

Today, June 27, 2014, Allen Grossman died.

After a long time, the voice of the man
Stops. It was good to talk on and on.
He rises. And the sea or forest becomes
A level way reaching to night and the
    thunder.

But, in fact, there is no night. There is
No thunder.

—

I remember speaking a word whose
meaning I didn't know but about
which I had some inkling, some intuition, then inserting that word into
a sentence, testing how it seemed to
fit or chafe against the context and
the syntax, rolling the word around,
as it were, on my tongue. I remember
my feeling that I possessed only part
of the meaning of the word, like one
of those fragmented friendship neck-
laces, and I had to find the other half in
the social world of speech. I remember

104

walking around as a child repeating a word I'd overheard, applying it wildly, and watching how, miraculously, I was rarely exactly wrong. If you are five and you point to a sycamore or an idle backhoe or a neighbor stooped over his garden or to images of these things on a television set and utter "vanish" or utter "varnish" you will never be only incorrect; if your parent or guardian is curious, she can find a meaning that makes you almost eerily prescient—the neighbor is dying, losing weight, or the backhoe has helped a structure disappear or is glazed with rain water or the sheen of spectacle lends to whatever appears onscreen a strange finish. To derive your understanding of a word by watching others adjust to your use of it: Do you remember the feeling that sense was provisional and that two people could build around an utterance a world in which any usage signified? I think

Vanish or varnish

that's poetry. And when I felt I finally mastered a word, when I could slide it into a sentence with a satisfying click, that wasn't poetry anymore—that was something else, something functional within a world, not the liquefaction of its limits.

Remember how easily our games could break down or reform or redescribe reality? The magical procedure was always first and foremost repetition: Every kid knows the phenomenon that psychologists call "semantic saturation," wherein a word is repeated until it feels emptied of sense and becomes mere sound—"to repeat, monotonously, some common word, until the sound, by dint of frequent repetition, ceased to convey any idea whatever to the mind," as Poe describes it in the story "Berenice." Your parents enforce a bedtime and, confined to your bed, you yell, "Bedtime" over and over again until whatever meaning seemed to dwell therein is banished along with all symbolic order, and you're a little feral animal underneath the glowing plastic stars. Linguistic repetition, you learn from an early age, can give form or take it away, because it forces a confrontation with the malleability of language and the world we build with it, build upon it. Most horrifying was to do this or have it done to your own name, worst of all by some phalanx of chanting kids on the playground—to be reminded how easily you could be expelled from the human community, little innominate snot-nosed feral animal too upset even to tattle. And what would you say? "They broke my name." The teacher would just instruct you to cast a weak spell back: "Sticks and stones may break my bones, but words ..."

We call these children's games, not children's work, but isn't a child

That's my name; don't wear it out.

precisely one who doesn't yet observe a clear distinction between what counts as labor and what counts as leisure? All children are poets in that sense. I'm asking you to locate your memory of that early linguistic instability, of language as a creative and destructive force. I have done the reading, and the reading suggests that we always experience this power as withdrawing from us, or we from it—if we didn't distance from this capacity it would signal our failure to be assimilated into the actual, adult world, i.e., we would be crazy. Our resentment of that falling away from poetry takes the form (among other forms) of contempt for grown-up poets and for poems; poets, who, by their very nature, accuse us of that distance, make it felt, but fail to close it.

I remember when the Hypermart opened in Topeka, a 235,000-square-foot big-box store with vast and towering aisles of brightly lit, brightly packaged goods, remember the cereal aisle in particular, "family sized" boxes of Cap'n Crunch repeating as far as the eye could see. And roller-skating —I'm not kidding—among these sugary infinities were young uniformed workers, uniformed both in the sense of wearing the costume of their franchise but also in the sense of uniformly following the conventions of teenage "beauty"—which was not beauty, but a sublimity of perfect exchangeability, the roller skates themselves a gesture, albeit dated, toward capital's lubricity. Every flake or piece of puffed corn belonging to me as good as belonged to you—Warhol is the Whitman of the actual: "A Coke is a Coke and no amount of money can get you a better Coke than the one the bum on the corner is drinking. All the Cokes are the same and all the Cokes are good." The same goodness, the good sameness:

Hypermart

The energy that coursed through me, undid me, at Hypermart—a store that was to the snot-nosed me what Mont Blanc was to Shelley—I consider that energy integral to poetry. "Poetry is a kind of money," Wallace Stevens said; like money, it mediates between the individual and the collective, dissolves the former into the latter, or lets the former reform out of the latter only to dissolve again. Do you remember that sense (or have it now) of being a tentative node in a limitless network of goods and flows? Because that's also poetry, albeit in a perverted form, wherein relations between people must appear as things. The affect of abstract exchange, the feeling that everything is fungible—what is its song? The actual song of my early youth might be eighties synthpop, but the impulse that gives rise to it, I maintain, is Poetry.

A Coke is a Coke is a Coke

Or that summer I was at Back to Nature Day Camp at Gage Park and there was a heat wave, and the confused teenaged counselors, in order to keep us from sunstroke, took us to see a one-dollar matinee at Gage 4 Theater five days in a row. I remember *Planet of the Apes*—all the younger campers wept with terror. I want to note only that each time the house lights dimmed— these were the first movies I'd ever seen in a theater without the emotional buffer of my family—I felt that other worlds were possible, felt all my senses had been reset and sharpened, that some of them were melding with those of the other kids with their giant Cokes in the dark beside me. This faded quickly as the film progressed and the image of a particular alternative world appeared before us on the screen; there was no trace of it by the time we were rereleased into the preternaturally bright day, but each time the lights went down and the first preview lit up the screen, I felt overwhelmed

The Nature Theater of Topeka

by an abstract capacity I associate with Poetry. Not the artwork itself—even when the artwork is great—but the little clearing the theater makes. (A few summers ago I attended an aggressively mediocre opera at a gorgeous outdoor theater in Santa Fe, and when my boredom had deepened into something like a trance, I happened to see from our distant seats a single firefly slowly flashing around the orchestra, then floating onto the stage, then drifting back beyond the proscenium: its light appearing here in New Mexico and then three leagues from Seville, here in clock time and there the hatred of poetry in the continuous present tense of art. Since then, I've been attending outdoor theater when I can, less interested in the particular play than in watching, say, a police helicopter over Central Park drift into the airspace over the Forest of Arden—while, back in the historical present, I like to imagine, the suspect escapes.)

It is on the one hand a mundane experience and on the other an experience of the structure behind the mundane, patches of unprimed canvas peeking through the real. And—why not speak of it—fucking and getting fucked up was part of it, is, the way sex and substances can liquefy the particulars of perception into an experience of form. The way a person's stutter can be liquefied by song.

There is no need to go on multiplying examples of an impulse that can produce no adequate examples—of a capacity that can't be objectified without falsification. I've written in its defense, and in defense of our denunciation of it, because that is the dialectic of a vocation no less essential for being impossible. All I ask the haters—and I, too, am one—is that they strive to perfect their contempt, even consider bringing it to bear on poems, where *For the* *genuine*

113

it will be deepened, not dispelled, and where, by creating a place for possibility and present absences (like unheard melodies), it might come to resemble love.

Also published by Fitzcarraldo Editions

Zone by Mathias Enard (Fiction)
Translated from French by Charlotte Mandell
'A modern masterpiece.'
— David Collard, *Times Literary Supplement*

Memory Theatre by Simon Critchley (Essay)
'A brilliant one-of-a-kind mind-game occupying
a strange frontier between philosophy, memoir
and fiction.'
— David Mitchell, author of *The Bone Clocks*

On Immunity by Eula Biss (Essay)
'A vaccine against vague and incoherent thinking.'
— Rebecca Solnit, author of *Wanderlust*

My Documents by Alejandro Zambra (Fiction)
Translated from Spanish by Megan McDowell
'Strikingly original.'
— James Wood, *New Yorker*

It's No Good by Kirill Medvedev (Essay)
Introduced by Keith Gessen
Translated by Keith Gessen, Mark Krotov,
Cory Merrill and Bela Shayevich
'Russia's first authentic post-Soviet writer.'
— Keith Gessen, co-founder of *n+1*

Street of Thieves by Mathias Enard (Fiction)
Translated from French by Charlotte Mandell
'This is what the great contemporary French
novel should be. ... Enard fuses the traditions
of Camus and Céline, but he is his own man.'
— Patrick McGuinness, author of *The Last Hundred Days*

Pond by Claire-Louise Bennett (Fiction)
'An extraordinary collection of short stories –
profoundly original though not eccentric, sharp
and tender, funny and deeply engaging. A very
new sort of writing...'
— Sara Maitland, author of *A Book of Silence*

Nicotine by Gregor Hens (Essay)
Introduced by Will Self
Translated from German by Jen Calleja
'A luminous and nuanced exploration of how
we're constituted by our obsessions, how our
memories arrange themselves inside of us, and
how – or if – we control our own lives.'
— Leslie Jamison, author of *The Empathy Exams*

Nocilla Dream by Agustín Fernández Mallo (Fiction)
Translated from Spanish by Thomas Bunstead
'There is something deeply strange and finally
unknowable to this book, in the very best way
a testament to the brilliance of Fernández Mallo.'
— Ben Marcus, author of *The Flame Alphabet*

Pretentiousness: Why It Matters by Dan Fox (Essay)
'Dan Fox makes a very good case for a re-evaluation
of the word "pretentious". The desire to be more
than we are shouldn't be belittled. Meticulously
researched, persuasively argued – where would
we be as a culture if no-one was prepared to risk
coming across as pretentious? *Absolument* nowhere,
darling – that's where.'
— Jarvis Cocker

Counternarratives by John Keene (Fiction)
'Keene's collection of short and longer historical
fictions are formally varied, mould-breaking
and deeply political. He's a radical artist working
in the most conservative genres, and any search
for innovation in this year's US fiction should
start here.'
— Christian Lorentzen, *Vulture*

Football by Jean-Philippe Toussaint (Essay)
Translated from French by Shaun Whiteside
'For any serious French writer who has come
of age during the last thirty years, one question
imposes itself above all others: what do you do
after the nouveau roman? ... Foremost among
this group, and bearing that quintessentially
French distinction of being Belgian, is
Jean-Philippe Toussaint.'
— Tom McCarthy, author of *Satin Island*

Second-hand Time by Svetlana Alexievich (Essay)
Translated from Russian by Bela Shayevich
'In this spellbinding book, Svetlana Alexievich
orchestrates a rich symphony of Russian voices
telling their stories of love and death, joy and
sorrow, as they try to make sense of the twentieth
century, so tragic for their country.'
— J. M. Coetzee

Fitzcarraldo Editions
243 Knightsbridge
London, SW7 1DN
United Kingdom

The Hatred of Poetry by Ben Lerner
Copyright © 2016 by Ben Lerner
Published by arrangement with Farrar, Straus and Giroux LLC,
18 West 18th Street, New York NY 10011 USA
All rights reserved
This edition first published in Great Britain
by Fitzcarraldo Editions in 2016

The right of Ben Lerner to be identified as the
author of this work has been asserted in accordance with
Section 77 of the Copyright, Designs and Patent Act 1988.

ISBN 978-1-910695-15-9

Design by Ray O'Meara
Typeset in Fitzcarraldo
Printed and bound by TJ International

Fitzcarraldo Editions